THE NEW HARTFORD MEMORIAL LIBRARY
P.O. Box 247
Central Avenue at Town Hill Road
New Hartford, Connecticut 06057
(860) 379-7235

WITHDRAWN

D1314646

★ SPORTS STARS ★

MONICA SELES
THE COMEBACK KID

BY MARK STEWART

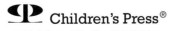 Children's Press®
A Division of Grolier Publishing
New York London Hong Kong Sydney
Danbury, Connecticut

Photo Credits
© : Allsport USA: 6, 45 right (Clive Brunskill), 26, 33, 42 bottom (Simon
Bruty), 8, 23 (Bob Martin); AP/Wide World Photos: 24, 27, 28, 29, 30, 34, 39;
Caryn Levy: 3, 10, 12, 13, 14, 44 right, 46; Corbis-Bettmann: 36, 45 left;
John Klein: 40; Reuters/Corbis-Bettmann: 35, 37; Russ Adams: 18, 44 left;
SportsChrome: 22 (Robert Tringali)

Library of Congress Cataloging-in-Publication Data

Stewart, Mark.
  Monica Seles : the comeback kid / by Mark Stewart.
    p. cm.–(Sports stars)
  Summary: Follows the life of the tennis star who became the
youngest winner of a Grand Slam title in over 100 years, from her
childhood in Yugoslavia through the traumatic attack at a match in
Germany in 1993 to her comeback in 1995.
    ISBN 0-516-20489-0 (lib. bdg.)   0-516-26054-5 (pbk.)
    1. Seles, Monica, 1973- –Juvenile literature. 2. Tennis
players–Yugoslavia–Biography–Juvenile literature.
    3. Women tennis players–Yugoslavia–Biography–Juvenile literature.
  [1. Seles, Monica, 1973-   . 2. Tennis players. 3. Women–Biography.]
  I. Title. II. Series.
GV994.S45S84   1997
796.342'092   96–48806
[B]–DC21   CIP
                                       AC

© 1997 by Children's Press,® Inc.
All rights reserved. Published simultaneously in Canada.
Printed in the United States of America.
1 2 3 4 5 6 7 8 9 10 R 06 05 04 03 02 01 00 99 98 97

★ CONTENTS ★

TWO-HANDED FOREHAND

Monica Seles holds her tennis racket loosely in her hands. Across the court, her opponent tosses a tennis ball into the air and makes a blistering serve. Concentrating on the flight of the ball, Monica watches as it clears the net and then turns her body as it bounces toward her. With a loud grunt, Monica uses both hands to whip the head of her racket toward the rising ball. The two-handed forehand propels the ball over the net and into the corner of the court. Her opponent is left motionless at the service line; the point goes to Seles. Monica allows herself a brief smile, then prepares to return the next serve.

Monica celebrates a winning shot.

Since her arrival on the tennis scene, Monica Seles has used her enormous power and unconventional style to win tournaments. But when she stood at the top of the tennis world, a madman with a knife nearly took it all away from her. Recently, however, she has courageously devoted herself to reclaiming her place as one of best tennis players in the world.

★ 2 ★

BEGINNING
IN YUGOSLAVIA

When five-year-old Monica Seles announced to her parents that she was not interested in tennis, they told her that was fine. If she did not enjoy herself on the court, there was no reason to continue playing. Besides, her older brother, Zoltan, was the player in the family. He was already one of the best young tennis players in Yugoslavia.

As the trophies piled up in her brother's room, Monica began to wonder if she had made the right decision. Finally, she asked her father to teach her how to play. Karolj Seles had studied physical education in college and enjoyed a brief

Karolj and Monica Seles

career as a track-and-field athlete, but tennis was new to him. When his children started to play tennis, he read everything he could find on the subject, added some of his own ideas, and began to teach.

The Seleses lived in Novi Sad, a town in the northern part of Yugoslavia, which is now part of Serbia. At the time, Yugoslavia was a socialist country, and "luxuries" such as tennis equipment were sometimes hard to come by. Monica's father had to make a ten-hour trip to Italy whenever one of his children needed a new racket!

Although Monica was very small, her father knew she was strong enough to play tennis. In fact, she could easily lift the weights that her brother used in his training, even though he was eight years older. "I had unbelievable strength for a little girl," she explains. "In our town the soda pop bottles had tops that were so difficult to open that neither my parents nor my brother could manage them. At the age of five years, I could pop the tops off with one hand."

Monica's father believed that his six-year-old daughter could do great things in tennis if she could learn to love the game. Sometimes, he placed cute little stuffed animals where he wanted Monica to hit the ball and told her she could keep them if she could strike them. To get her to swing as hard as she could, he would draw Jerry, the cartoon mouse, on the ball and tell Monica to pretend she was Tom, the cartoon cat.

Even though she was a small girl, Monica could hit the ball with a lot of power.

He would also sketch pictures of a rabbit called Little Mo on a thick pad of paper, then flip the pages quickly to make the character appear to move. Little Mo showed Monica the proper way to hit the ball and helped to correct flaws in her game. "My father's animated cartoons really helped me learn the right service motion," Monica claims. "For example, if I

To encourage Monica to hit harder, her father drew a small mouse on the ball.

was leaning too far back, or my behind was sticking out, he'd draw Mo serving that way. Then he'd draw the correct version so that I could see the difference. And because he used cartoons and lots of humor, I always enjoyed practicing."

Monica's backhand generates tremendous power.

After just a few months of practice, Monica had mastered one of the most difficult skills in tennis: she could hit the ball on the rise. This meant that she did not have to stay back and engage in long rallies. She could squeeze off shots from anywhere on the court. To add power to her strokes, Monica's father taught her to hit both her forehand and backhand by holding the racket with both hands. This two-handed grip was—and still is—considered a very unusual approach.

Monica entered her first tournament when she was six. She was so new to the game that she was not even sure how to keep score. She would glance at her father during her matches, not for coaching advice, but to see if she was winning! Still, she reached the semifinals and won her first trophy. Soon, she would have even more trophies than her brother.

**Monica (right) and a friend at the Orange Bowl junior
tournament, 1985**

* 3 *

COMING TO AMERICA

Monica was just nine years old when she won the Yugoslavian 12-and-under championship in 1983. A year later, she won the European 12-and-under title. In 1985, Monica won the European title again, and she was named her country's Sportswoman of the Year. No one under the age of 18 ever had earned this honor before.

In 1985, she traveled to the Orange Bowl tournament in Miami, Florida, where she competed against the best junior players in the world. Monica played stunning tennis on her way to the 12-and-under title, and in the process, caught the eye of tennis coach Nick Bollettieri.

In Florida, Monica attracted the attention of Nick Bollettieri (right).

    Bollettieri ran a tennis academy in Bradenton, Florida, and had a reputation for turning out top players. He invited Monica to stay and play at the academy for two weeks, free of charge. Monica accepted his offer and had a great time. A year later, Bollettieri offered her a full scholarship. In Monica, he saw a chance to mold a future champion. In Nick, Monica saw an

opportunity to take her game—and her family—
to the next level. An agreement was made to send
Monica and Zoltan to the academy.

Life at the Bollettieri Academy kept Monica
very busy. There were new kids to meet, new
coaches to work with, a new school to attend, and
a new language to learn. At first, it was all fun
and very exciting. But soon, Monica believed she
had made a horrible mistake. The academy
coaches told her to give up her two-handed
forehand, and her entire game began to fall
apart. She was now losing to players she had
once beaten easily, and she did not understand
why.

Monica and Zoltan spoke to their parents
by telephone every Saturday, but she never
mentioned the problems she was having. Monica
kept the truth from her mother and father for
five months, until she could not stand it any
longer. She told them that if they could not
come and stay with her, she wanted to go home.

"I desperately missed my mom and dad," Monica explains. "I was just a kid, lost in a country where I couldn't understand the language. The only reason I'd come to the academy was for my tennis game, and I was playing terribly."

Monica's parents left their jobs and flew to Florida. When her father saw what the coaches had done to his daughter's game, he was outraged. He instructed Monica to return to the way she had been playing before, and he also changed her training routine. Her game returned, and her mood improved dramatically.

Karolj Seles and Nick Bollettieri did agree on one very important thing: Monica would not play any matches until she was ready to join the women's tennis tour. "Taking the pressure off helped me develop more," she says. "I could work on all kinds of new things and never worry about winning or losing."

Monica practices at the Bollettieri Academy.

After joining the tour, Monica challenged tennis legend Chris Evert (left).

By March 1988, everyone agreed it was time for Monica to try her luck on the women's tour. In a tournament at Boca Raton, Florida, she met her first professional opponent, Helen Kelesi. Monica battled to win the first set in a tiebreaker, but nearly lost her concentration in the second set when superstars Chris Evert, Steffi Graf, and Gabriela Sabatini sat down in the stands to watch her play. Monica defeated Kelesi, then nearly overpowered Evert in their second-round match. The very next week, she almost beat Sabatini.

The tennis world was stunned. Who was this girl? Where did she come from? How did she learn to hit that hard? Fans could not believe their eyes . . . or their ears. Monica hit with such force that she let out a piercing "Eeeee-yah!" every time she met the ball. No one had ever seen a woman hit that hard, and Monica was just going to get bigger and stronger.

Monica shocked the tennis world with her loud screeches when hitting the ball.

Monica receives her prize for winning a tournament.

★ 4 ★

TRIUMPH AND TRAGEDY

Monica Seles turned professional in February 1989 at a tournament in Washington, D.C. She reached the semifinals by beating three top players without losing a set. But then she could not continue because of a sprained ankle. Two months later, she beat Chris Evert in the final of a tournament in Houston, Texas.

Monica reached the semifinals of the 1989 French Open, where she nearly defeated the world's number-one player, Steffi Graf. She did well at Wimbledon and the U.S. Open, too, and finished with a number-six ranking. By all accounts, it was a great first year.

Monica won her first major event in the spring of 1990, when she ripped through her opponents to capture the Lipton International. The following weekend, she won an event in San Antonio, Texas. Monica was on a roll. She won her next tournament and then flew to Rome for the Italian Open. There she dominated all of her opponents, including Martina Navratilova, whom she beat 6–1, 6–1 in the final.

Monica reaches for a ball at the 1989 U.S. Open.

★ ★ ★

Monica (right) overpowered tennis legend Martina Navratilova (left) to win the Italian Open.

When asked what it was like to lose to Monica, Martina answered that she felt as if she had been run over by a truck. "The quickest match I ever played," Monica says of the Italian Open final. "Every shot was a winner and I had no inhibitions, held back nothing."

Monica lunges for a ball during the 1990 French Open.

After a little more than a year on the tour, Monica had defeated every top player except one: Steffi Graf. Facing the German superstar in the final of the 1990 German Open, Monica beat the world's top-ranked player on her "home turf," 6–4, 6–3. At the tour's next stop, the French Open, she again faced Graf in the final.

This time, Monica made a marvelous comeback to win the first-set tiebreaker and easily captured the second set. At the age of 16, Monica was the youngest winner of a Grand Slam title in more than one hundred years!

Monica, flanked by her mother and father, displays her French Open trophy.

Monica shakes hands with Steffi Graf after defeating Graf in the French Open.

★ ★ ★

Two stunning victories over Graf made Monica the most talked-about player in tennis. This did not please a German man named Günther Parche, who considered himself Steffi Graf's greatest fan. Parche sent letters, flowers, and money to Graf. He videotaped all of her matches and covered his walls with huge photos of her. When Graf won, he was thrilled; when she lost, he sometimes thought about suicide. Günther Parche was already a deeply troubled man. Over the next few years, Monica's success would push him over the edge.

In 1991, Monica won the Australian Open to become the youngest champion in the tournament's history. Then she fulfilled her lifelong dream by becoming the top-ranked player in the world. It happened on March 11, which meant that Monica—at 17 years, three months, and nine days—was the youngest woman ever to hold that honor. Over the next two years, Monica stayed in the top spot, winning the U.S.,

French, and Australian Opens two times each. In all, she captured 21 singles titles in 24 months.

Monica was looking forward to another great year in 1993. But Günther Parche had other plans. Disturbed by Steffi Graf's number-two ranking, he decided that the only way to restore his queen to her throne was to get rid of the woman who blocked her path. He bought a ticket to Monica's quarterfinal match at the Citizen Cup in Hamburg, Germany, then worked his way to the edge of the stands. While the players were changing ends, Parche positioned himself at the railing, just a few feet from where he knew Monica would stop to sit and take a sip of water. When she did, he pulled a 9-inch knife from a bag and tried to plunge it into her back. As Parche made his desperate lunge, someone screamed, causing Monica to shift forward an inch or two in her chair—not much, but enough to save her life. The knife went an inch and a half into her back, just below her left shoulder blade.

Monica coils her body to produce a powerful serve.

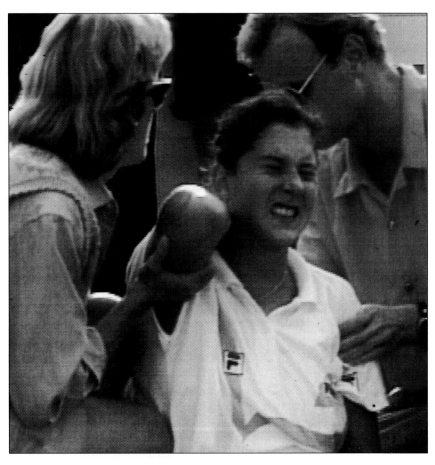

Monica grimaces as she feels the wound in her back.

"It was a sudden, sharp burning point on the left that radiated pain across my back and down my right side," she remembers. "I looked back over my left shoulder and saw a man in a baseball cap holding a bloody knife in both hands. He raised his arms above his head to strike again."

Luckily, a security guard grabbed Parche and knocked the knife from his hands. Monica took a few steps and collapsed.

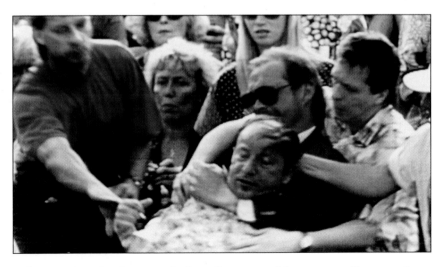

Günther Parche is wrestled to the ground by a security guard.

Monica shows the strain of the attack at a press conference.

Later that evening, the tennis world breathed a sigh of relief. News from the hospital was encouraging. The knife had not penetrated Monica's lung, and it had done relatively little physical damage. Emotionally, however, Monica was a wreck. It made her ill to think that someone had actually tried to kill her.

The wound to Monica's back would heal in a couple of months. But the scar it left went far deeper. Just days after the attack, the Women's Tennis Association announced that Monica would not be able to keep her number-one ranking while she recovered. She—along with her fans—found this horrible. "I lay in my hospital bed thinking: Günther Parche got just what he wanted," she recalls. "Steffi Graf will be number one in a few weeks, and I'm out of the game."

During the rest of 1993, Monica spent most of her time in rehabilitation. By year's end, she had regained a full range of motion, and rumors

began to circulate that she was ready to rejoin the tour in 1994. But in early January, she announced that she would not be coming back. Some believe the attack on figure skater Nancy Kerrigan made Monica nervous.

Monica's cause for worry grew when she heard of the 1994 attack on Nancy Kerrigan (above), another prominent athlete.

Others say she was distressed about her father, who had been diagnosed with cancer a few weeks earlier. The fact that Parche had gone to trial that fall and received little more than a slap on the wrist also contributed to her deep sadness and confusion.

Monica vowed not to play tennis again until it made her happy. Meanwhile, her weight rose from 140 pounds to nearly 180. "The only constants in my life were food, fear, and depression," she recalls. Finally, in the early months of 1995, Monica's spirits began to brighten. She had developed a friendship with Martina Navratilova, who had experienced plenty of ups and downs during her long career. Martina and Monica played a little and talked a lot, and soon Monica was feeling like she was ready to come back. When the Women's Tennis Association heard that Monica might return, she was told that her ranking would be restored, and that she and Steffi Graf would be "co-number ones."

Monica and Martina Navratilova share a hug after a match.

Monica was thrilled to be playing professional tennis again.

★ 5 ★

THE COMEBACK

In August 1995, Monica entered the Canadian Open, her first tournament in more than 27 months. She had worked hard to get back in shape, but until she actually stepped onto the court, she could not be sure whether she was ready or not.

What convinced Monica Seles to rejoin the tennis tour? "For a long time after the stabbing, everything was so serious—just dark colors and hard decisions," she explains. "I said to myself, 'Monica, you can't let this experience take away the kid side of you, because that's what life is about.'"

Monica began her comeback by winning the 1995 Canadian Open.

Monica's first Grand Slam victory in her comeback was the Australian Open.

★ ★ ★

In one of the most remarkable comeback stories in sports, Monica won the Canadian Open. She defeated Gabriela Sabatini in the semifinals, and then blew Amanda Coetzer off the court in a 6–1, 6–0 final. In all, Monica beat five top players, losing a total of just 14 games, to set a Canadian Open record. After reaching the final of the 1995 U.S. Open, Monica won her first Grand Slam event of 1996, the Australian Open. There, she ran her unbeaten string in that tournament to a record 28 matches.

As the rest of the year unfolded, Monica had her share of wins and losses. She battled injuries and exhaustion, and tried her best to survive the pressures of being the most recognized figure in women's sports. But deep down, she loved every minute of it. After two long years, she finally was able to do the thing she cherished most: going onto a court and playing great tennis.

C ☆ H ☆ R ☆ O ☆ N

1973 • Monica is born in Novi Sad, Yugoslavia.

1983 • Monica wins the 12-and-under tournament in Yugoslavia.

1984-85 • Monica wins the European 12-and-under tournament for the second time in a row. She is voted her country's Sportswoman of the Year.

1985 • Tennis coach Nick Bollettieri invites Monica to attend his academy in Florida.

1988 • Monica plays in her first professional tournament.

1989 • At age 15, Monica reaches the semifinals of the French Open.

O ★ L ★ O ★ G ★ Y

1991 • Monica becomes second-youngest U.S. Open champion at age 17.

1993 • In Hamburg, Germany, Monica is stabbed by Günther Parche. Monica withdraws from competition and suffers from depression.

1994 • Monica becomes a U.S. citizen.

1995 • After 27 months, Monica returns to tennis and wins the Canadian Open.

1996 • Monica leads U.S. team to Federation Cup victory.

MONICA SELES

MONICA SELES

Place of Birth
Novi Sad, Yugoslavia

Date of Birth
December 2, 1973

Height
5' 10 1/2"

Weight
145 pounds

WTA World Champion
1991 & 1992

★ GRAND SLAM CHAMPIONSHIPS ★

Australia Open	French Open	U.S. Open
1991	1990	1991
1992	1991	1992
1993	1992	
1996		

★ ★ ★

ABOUT THE AUTHOR

Mark Stewart grew up in New York City in
the 1960s and 1970s—when the Mets, Jets, and
Knicks all had championship teams. As a child,
Mark read everything about sports he could lay
his hands on. Today, he is one of the busiest
sportswriters around. Since 1990, he has written
close to 500 sports stories for kids, including
profiles on more than 200 atheletes, past and
present. A graduate of Duke University, Mark
served as senior editor of *Racquet*, a national
tennis magazine, and was managing editor
of *Super News*, a sporting goods industry
newspaper. He is the author of Grolier's
All-Pro Biography series, and four titles
in the Children's Press Sports Stars series.

THE NEW HARTFORD MEMORIAL LIBRARY
P.O. Box 247
Central Avenue at Town Hill Road
New Hartford, Connecticut 06057
(860) 379-7235